positive impact . . .

praise from top leaders and mentors

"Everyone needs a mentor to get you to the next level. This fast-moving book is an entertaining and helpful blueprint for you to follow."

Brian Tracy, Best-selling Author
Create Your Own Future

"Over the course of my career, I have been blessed with a number of mentors. The advice offered in this book is priceless because it is genuine, sincere, and powerfully helpful to anyone who wants to improve their life."

Bill Bartmann, Author
Billionaire Secrets to Success

"Sure wish I would have understood and embraced these simple truths when I was 22 years old."

Todd Milano, President
Central Pennsylvania College

"A fantastic example of success. This book is truly 'Tremendous'."

Jack Mates
Former President and CEO of Velcro USA

"Simple wisdom that's tremendously powerful. I dare you to read this book and not take away a few pearls that immediately rock your world."

Bob Scheinfeld, Founder of The Ultimate Lifestyle Academy
#1 Best-selling Author, *The 11th Element*

"This book will force you to see how you can have anything in life you truly want. It will have an enormously *Positive Impact* on the way you look at your business and personal life."

John Assaraf, a.k.a. The Street Kid Speaker
#1 Best-selling Author, *Financial Aerobics*

"Not since the *One Minute Manager* have I read as powerful a parable as *Positive Impact* ... distilled volumes of text on team building and ethical business practices into an easy-to-read, informative, inspirational, and very motivating book. It's a must for all who want to better themselves and their team's productivity."

David M. Corbin, Speaker
Author, *Psyched on Service, Brandslaughter, Illuminate*

"This thought-provoking fable is a masterpiece ... a real gem that's easy to read and leaves you searching for ways to proactively make a difference in other people's lives."

Randy Gilbert
Host of TheInsideSuccessShow.com

"*Positive Impact* hits a multitude of areas that are lacking in particularly the youngsters in the workforce today. This book tactfully engages the reader and allows both the apprentice and the mentor to relate to the responsibility of leading and the learning of humble following."

Rick Prohm, Automotive Sales Trainer
Sydney, Australia

"If you're going for the gold in your personal and professional life, *Positive Impact* is a must read. This gem is filled with time proven principles that will take you to the top!"

Ruben Gonzalez
Olympian, Speaker, and Author of *The Courage to Succeed*

"...will leave you with a POWERFUL message while having a *Positive Impact* toward the way you think about running your business."

Mike Litman, #1 Best-selling Co-author
Conversations with Millionaires

"*Positive Impact* is inspiring and practical. Set in a delightful story, it illustrates what living with passion and purpose can do. Read it once — read it twice more. Be inspired and spread your inspiration. That is a life well lived. Bravo!"

Mary Goulet, Radio Talk Show Host,
Author of *MomsTown Guide to Getting a Life*
(Hyperion Books 2005)

"What an impact the principles in this book possess! And the way the reader is taught the principles makes it have—yes, you guessed it—quite an impact! This is such a tremendously engaging read, you're hoping nothing interrupts you."

W. Karl Parker, President
Health and Wealth Resource Foundation

"The message from *Positive Impact* is clear ... have a mentor! It is interesting that all of them encourage me to read more. If you are new to reading positive books, *Positive Impact* has the message you need to develop your thinking for greater success."

George Peintner, President
Word Information Network

"I like practical, proven ideas. In *Positive Impact,* the authors provide a book filled with such ideas. As you read the book you will say, 'why didn't I think of that?' Buy the book, read it with a highlighter, and then make a difference in your life and the lives of those around you by implementing what you highlighted."

John Segal, President
North American Products Corporation

"*Positive Impact* reminds us that each obstacle we face presents an opportunity to summit our fears and gain courage to move forward."

Dean Cardinale, Mt. Everest Summiteer

"The lessons developed in this wonderful book contain many principles. This will be another winner for those readers seeking a road map for changing their life and the lives of those around them."

Walt DeVault, SVP
Lee Hecht Harrison

"*Positive Impact* reminds us that the task doesn't bring dignity to the doer, it's the doer who brings dignity to the task! Therefore, there is no such thing as a menial task."

Jim Mudd Sr., CEO
Mudd Group

"Charlie and Greg make a great team! *Positive Impact* sets new standards in the crowded self-help market by sharing that anyone can realize success, simply by helping others achieve their goals."

Denis Waitley
Best-selling Author

positive
impact

the secret to making a world of difference

GREG S. REID
CHARLIE "TREMENDOUS" JONES
TRACEY C. JONES

Positive Impact
The Secret to Making a World of Difference
Greg S. Reid, Charlie "Tremendous" Jones, Tracey C. Jones

Copyright © 2021

Third Edition
ISBN: 978-1-7351657-4-5

JOINT VENTURE

Joint Venture Publishing
Blue Sky R&D, LLC

Printed in the United States of America

dedication

To all those who make a *Positive Impact* on others' lives—the *mentors, parents, coaches, teachers, and dreamers.*

hank you to all of our friends and family—*"You have made a Positive Impact in our lives, which will always be remembered."*

Contents

Introduction   13

Treat Everyone Equally   17

We ARE the Company We Keep   29

Be a Star!   39

Mentoring Your Way to Million$ 51

A Positive Attitude Gets Results   59

It Doesn't Matter Who Gets the Credit   67

Wake Up and Live the Life You Love   73

Welcome to the Family!   85

Universal Success Secrets   89

Share Your Success Stories   93

About Greg S. Reid   95

About Charlie "Tremendous" Jones   97

About Tracey C. Jones   99

introduction

This book is a compilation of stories derived from our business experiences. Each was reconfigured to fit into this parable that describes real life events, which shaped our outlook on life and business success.

"All I want in life is to give my life my all."
Greg S. Reid

"You are the same today you'll be in five years,
except for the people you meet and the books you read...
`Charlie "Tremendous" Jones

"Never underestimate the power of your influence
in shaping another's life."
Tracey C. Jones

treat everyone equally

-equally nice!

treat everyone equally

"Monday mornings get here way too fast," complained the 35-year-old executive to the woman behind the desk.

"You must be John Bishop. Mr. Cams will be with you shortly," responded the smartly- dressed lady, who then motioned for the younger man to take a seat.

"Thank you," he said as he pulled his phone out of his pocket and walked toward the sofa.

"I'm sorry we don't have any reading material. But I'll be happy to keep you company. Would you like to talk?" the woman asked kindly.

The young man didn't know how to reply. No one had ever asked him a question like that before, especially not someone so low on the totem pole. As a receptionist, the fact that she was attempting to make small talk with him was surprising. Like a deer caught in the headlights, he was stunned and unsure how to respond.

"Ummm, ahhh, that's okay. I have a few things to tend to. Thanks, anyway," he added as an afterthought as he continued to go through his phone in obvious avoidance.

"Very well," the friendly woman said, flashing a friendly smile. "If there's anything you need, just ask. By the way, what can I get you to drink? We have coffee, iced tea, soda, and water."

"Uhhh, nothing," the young man said, brushing her off once again. Annoyed and feeling even more uncomfortable than before, he thought, *Why the heck is this lady trying to talk to me? I mean, doesn't she know who I am?*

John was one of those cocky people who thinks status is everything. To him, what people do for a living, where they live, which clubs they join, and the size of their portfolios all indicate who they are as people. He snubs those he feels are insignificant and common. In his mind, the only people who were worthy of his time were powerful, rich, successful, and had the kind of clout and connections to help him get that way, too.

That's why he was there today. He'd read numerous articles about 65-year-old Oscar Cams, the CEO of a major manufacturing company and the most respected entrepreneur in town. Everyone described Cams as the epitome of success; everything he touched seemed to turn to gold. John, feeling dissatisfied with his own career, despite his quick rise to executive VP, wanted to pick the older man's brain and learn the secrets to his success. *Why does everyone rave about this guy? What makes him so special? How come he seems so happy and passionate about what he's doing, while I feel exactly the opposite?* Those are the questions he wanted answered and the reason he wanted to meet the admired entrepreneur, not to chit chat with a receptionist he didn't care to know.

Interrupting his thoughts yet again, the woman behind the desk asked, "Do you have any pets, Mr. Bishop?"

"Look," he snapped condescendingly, "I'm here to meet with your boss, and I've been waiting over a month for this appointment. Can't you just let me be for a while so I can prepare for this meeting?"

Before the polite woman could respond, an older, very fit, extremely energetic man popped his head out of an office door and said in a cheerful tone, "Hi! You must be John, the superstar vice president I've been hearing so much about. Come on into my office." Waving his arm toward the reception desk, he added, "By the way, did you get a chance to meet my wife, Ellen?"

Once again, John was caught off guard. Stopping in mid step, he froze, wishing someone would put him out of his misery. Looking once again like a deer caught in the headlights, he tried to think of a way out of what had quickly turned into an awkward situation. Then, the woman spoke up.

"Yes, dear," she replied, as John cringed at the irony of hearing her say, "Yes, *deer*."

"Fantastic! Then come on in and let's get started," the successful businessman proposed.

As a remorseful John walked through the solid oak doorway into Mr. Cams's office, he turned back to apologize, but Ellen raised her finger to her lips and gave him a hushed "Shhhh," and a slight, but obvious, wink of an eye. Her quickness in forgiving his rudeness made John realize that he probably wasn't the first to make such a bad impression. With a sense of relief, he gratefully smiled at her and mouthed a silent, "Thank you."

As the young VP entered the room, he quickly forgot his

embarrassment and shame. Taking in his surroundings, his face lit up like a child in a toy store.

It was as if he'd walked back in time and stepped into an old movie house, complete with refurbished theater chairs and classic film posters hanging above them—*Guys and Dolls, Casablanca, Singin' in the Rain.* As he marveled at his surroundings, John was sure he smelled the faint aroma of popcorn in the air. Mr. Cams's desk and chair sat in front of a giant window that was flanked on each side by red velvet draperies. While it resembled a big screen at the cinema, the draperies were actually framing a large panel of clear, shiny glass.

The view from the window revealed the inner workings of the host's factory, with people scurrying about among a conglomeration of humming machinery. It reminded John of the ant farm that fascinated him as a child. He'd spent hours on the outside looking in, watching the ants work in the sand between two panels of glass. It was a glimpse into another world, one that was separate from him, but totally visible.

"Wow!" he exclaimed. "This is not what I expected!"

"What did you expect?" asked Mr. Cams.

"With your prestige, I envisioned a large corner office, private and far removed from the day-to-day operations—impressive, but in a different way. At the risk of being inappropriate and unprofessional, I have to tell you, Mr. Cams, this place is awesome! My grandfather would have loved it!"

"Who was your grandfather?" the older gentleman inquired.

"Jacob Bishop. He used to run—" John's explanation was cut short when the older gentleman piped in and finished his sentence.

"The Three Palm Theater down on Market Street!" shouted Mr. Cams in obvious excitement. "He was a GREAT man! One of our first customers, in fact. Whatever happened to that old theater, anyway? That place was fantastic."

"My dad inherited it when my grandfather passed away," John replied. "Dad promised to rebuild it one day, but that day never came and now it just sits empty. I always hoped to reopen it one day in my grandfather's honor."

"Now, that's a great idea," replied the older gentleman. "I'd love to hear about your plans sometime. For now, have a seat and let's hear what else is on your mind."

Taking a chair, though, the younger guest found that he couldn't keep his eyes off the window and all the action.

"I suppose it's difficult for new visitors to stay focused with such a show before them," John observed.

"It's funny you use the word *show* to describe my family here," Mr. Cams replied.

"Family?"

"Yes, but before we cross that bridge, let me ask you why you've been working so hard to meet with me. I have to tell you, I appreciate your moxie, young man. Your persistence was quite impressive, and I've heard good things about you. So, share with me, what can I do for you?"

"Well, it's like this," the visitor explained. "As you may have heard, I've done pretty well these past few years, becoming a VP with my company and all. However, I feel as though I'm capped out, like I hit a self-imposed glass ceiling of sorts, and I can't progress. I was wondering—well, hoping really—if you could help me figure out what I'm doing wrong."

"You seem like a bright young man, John, and I seriously doubt that you don't know *exactly* what you're doing wrong." The student sat dumbfounded, unsure what the older man was referring to as he continued. "I'm sure I can show you a few more things you could be doing right, though."

"I don't get it. What's the difference?" asked John, genuinely interested.

"It's like this," said Mr. Cams. "You've achieved a high level of success. I'm sure you've done that by making a great number of good decisions, but none of us make good decisions all the time.

"Let me ask you this, John—do you like what you're doing? Do you have a real passion for it? I'm willing to bet the answer is no."

"How do you know?" asked the young entrepreneur.

"Because I was once just like you," admitted the mentor. "I thought I knew everything when I was your age, but the one thing I didn't know was what I wanted to do with my life. I had great success in most things I did, but I had no real excitement for them."

The younger man listened intently and nodded. "That's exactly where I am, Mr. Cams," he replied.

"So, to tell you the things you're doing *wrong* would be a waste of time and energy for both of us. What I can offer you, instead, are some ideas of what more you could do *right* and provide you with a glimpse into our family here. By sharing with you *my* passion, perhaps I can shine some light on a few ideas you can apply to your business. In the process, you might find your passion, like I did."

"That sounds great," beamed the eager student.

"But before we begin, you have to promise me one thing in regard to what I share with you."

"To keep it a secret between us, I bet," John quickly surmised.

"No! Heavens *no*," Mr. Cams laughed. "I want you to promise me the complete opposite. Everything I share with you, you *must* share with at least one other person."

The young entrepreneur sat in silence, the expression on his face similar to that of Mr. Spock in a *Star Trek* episode—one eyebrow quizzically higher than the other.

"Wellll, okaaay," John agreed, sounding a little befuddled.

"Great!" boomed his mentor. "Come back in the morning at 0700 hours. We'll go from there. Be sure to lose that tie and wear comfortable shoes. We're a hands-on environment here."

"Outstanding," acknowledged the pupil, reaching out to Mr. Cams to shake his hand in appreciation.

"Nonsense," replied Mr. Cams as he walked around his desk and gave John a good old-fashioned bear hug.

The startled newcomer stood in disbelief for a moment, wondering if he was imagining things. Was he in a movie, or did what he thought just happened really happen?

Then, as John turned to leave, Mr. Cams asked, "By the way, young man, did you learn one of the first new things to do right today?"

The young man faced his adviser and with a look of uncertainty, admitted, "I must have missed it. What was it?"

"*It* is right outside that door. I always keep the intercom on before I meet with someone new, so I can hear how they treat people other than me. If you'd known the woman at the reception desk is my wife, you probably would have been more cordial, don't you think?"

The young man's face turned red as he regretfully admitted, "Yes— yes, I would have."

"Well, there you go," Mr. Cams responded. "Look at the banner hanging above the doorway to my office, John. I think maybe you missed that, too."

Following the older man's instructions, John stuck his head out the door, looked up, and read the banner hanging there:

> Treat Everyone Equally—Equally Nice!

Mr. Cams continued, "The first thing to do right is to treat *everyone* equally—equally nice—because you don't know who the person next to you at a ballgame, in an elevator, driving alongside your car, or even sitting at the reception desk of a large corporation might be. Would you like to learn a way to treat everyone equally nice?"

"I'm all ears," said John.

"The most important thing you can do is take time to talk to people," revealed Mr. Cams, "just like I'm doing here with you today. Instead of being totally absorbed in *yourself* and *your* busy life and that phone in your hand, take time to look up and talk to the people you come in contact with each day. Don't just fly by with a quick hello. Stop and talk. You can learn a lot from talking to people. Do you have time for a quick story, John?"

"You bet!" the student answered, now quite fascinated by his mentor's approach and pleased that Mr. Cams is spending so much time with him.

"A man I know, who goes by the initials G.R., started a company in a little business park—a low-budget kind of place for startups. Across the hall from him was a group of older gentlemen who ran an organization called the Distinguished Flying Cross Society.

"Well, after months went by with G.R. just nodding a friendly hello their way, bumping into the guys in the hallway, and whatnot, he finally went over to see what these fellows were all about.

"Knocking at the door, he found their leader, a man named Jack, kneeling on the floor and shuffling some papers. Wearing one of those tweed jackets with leather patches on the elbows, Jack looked like a former college professor.

"As G.R. leaned inside the doorway just outside the office, he discovered that those older gentlemen were a hoot. They were pilots who'd flown in combat and survived to tell their stories. Each had received the Distinguished Flying Cross, an Armed Forces medal awarded for heroism or extraordinary achievement. They were heroes in every sense of the word, and they'd started their society to publicize the meaning of the award and to honor its recipients. In addition, they established scholarships, arranged reunions, conducted tours, and much more.

"As they spoke, G.R. couldn't help but wonder about Jack. He said, 'I have to tell you, this organization you run is absolutely the best. What's your background? How do you hold everything together so well? I mean, did you manage a business, teach business courses, or do something like that before doing this?'

"Jack, without blinking, looked up at the visitor standing in the doorway and simply said, 'You could say that.'

"'Well, what was it? Did you manage or teach?' G.R. pressed further.

"'I ran a company,' Jack said with pride.

"'Was it a big company? Were you the GM, VP, or what?' G.R. continued.

"In an authoritative voice, Jack replied, 'I'd say it was a company that started small, with a *big* idea, and turned into a large corporation after many years of trial and error.' Still shuffling through the scattered papers, Jack continued, 'The title I held was one of many. You see, son, when you're immersed in your passion, doing what you love and believe in, the words beneath your name on your stationery don't really matter. What we're doing here right now at this moment is what means the most, not the title that goes with it. But, with that said, in the business world I suppose I was considered the CEO.'

"G.R. stood there for a moment. He'd been preparing to hand his gold-leafed business card—with his title larger than his name—to this man. Instead, he put it back in his pocket. With his head lowered and his ego in check, he suddenly felt silly and let out a deep sigh.

"Snickering softly, feeling a little deflated, but yet open to learning more, he said, 'I think I need to go burn my business cards. Then I'd like to take you out to lunch someday so you can hand down more of your words of wisdom to me. I'm new at this game, and I'd greatly appreciate any input you're willing to pass along. Can we do that sometime soon?'

"'Sure, let's shoot for tomorrow,' Jack suggested. "G.R. literally beamed with excitement. 'Great!' he said. As he turned to leave Jack's patriotically decorated red-white-and-blue office, the rookie stammered out this fateful question to his new friend, 'By the way, what was the name of the company you ran, Jack?'

"Still shuffling through the papers on his floor, Jack quickly looked up and asked, 'Have you ever heard of Velcro?'"

John was floored. "Wow, Mr. Cams! What a great story and lesson. Thank you for sharing that with me," he said.

"And one day," continued Mr. Cams, "*you* might be that person passing along *your* words of wisdom."

With that, their first meeting came to an end. John had already learned decidedly more than he expected. He *thought* he knew everything before meeting Mr. Cams, but now realized just how wrong he'd been. It was a surprising outcome to this much anticipated meeting, and John walked away thinking tomorrow couldn't come soon enough.

we ARE the
company we keep

"Good morning, Mrs. Cams," said our young friend, John, as he walked into the office with a completely different attitude than the day before.

"Hello, Mr. Bishop. May I get you something?" the sharply dressed Mrs. Cams once again offered in her friendly tone.

"No, thank you. I want to say I'm sorry about the way I acted yesterday and ..."

Before John could finish his apology, Mr. Cams flew out of his office door like a freight train that had fallen off its tracks. "Come along— let's go!" he said, steaming full force past John and the reception desk.

"You'd better get going, John," urged Mrs. Cams, "or you'll never catch up."

Noticing John's startled look, she shouted, "Run!" pointing in the direction of Mr. Cams's exit.

As the young man John scrambled to catch up to his leader, he watched him stop to pick up a candy wrapper by a trash can. Rushing to his side, John blurted out, "Why are *you* doing this? Let's get a janitor!"

Mr. Cams stood and, looking his mentee in the eye, said, "Here's a quiz for you, John. Say you have some VIPs coming to your office and the cleaning staff didn't make it in the night before. The bathrooms are a mess, and the trash cans are full, but you want to make a good impression. Do you (a) call the cleaning crew and chew them out, (b) leave it—because it's not your job, or (c) clean it yourself?"

John froze on the spot. Once again, the protege was surprised and a little embarrassed by Mr. Cams's savvy, yet humble, demeanor. "Well," he stammered, feeling a little like he was back in elementary school, "I guess since I'm the VP of the corporation, I would ask someone else to do it."

"That's a shame," sighed Mr. Cams, shaking his head in disappointment. "You'll never be a leader with that kind of thinking."

"Why not? What are you talking about? I already *am* a leader. Remember my company? I'm the Senior Executive VP of a highly successful advertising firm."

"Just because you have a big title and pay people to do what you say, that doesn't make you a leader. You can't be a leader if no one follows," Mr. Cams warned.

"*Real* leaders do whatever it takes, whenever and wherever needed, without question or hesitation. The best leaders are those who are humble and care about others. A title and money won't gain you respect—or friends. Both must be earned."

John stood in silence as Mr. Cams continued. "Right here, right now, I would gladly roll up my sleeves and empty the trash, make the coffee, train the new guy—whatever task needs to be done. You see, my staff aren't just employees; they are my family."

"Wow, I don't know what to say," muttered John. "I guess I'm not used to this environment."

"You mean where leaders and employees have mutual respect and admiration for each other? Let me tell you a story. I came into work late one night, John. The man who cleans at night (we call him Pop) was sick, and his son, Charlie, was here cleaning. I asked Charlie why he came in, and he said his dad had sent him, saying, 'I don't want to let the family down.'

"You know what? That kid and I stayed here all night scrubbing this place together from top to bottom, just as Pop would have. When we finished, I swore Charlie to secrecy so no one would know he and I had done the work.

"That was two years ago, and Charlie is now my shipping department manager. His father has retired, but Pop will always be treated like family. Do you get the picture now, John?"

"Sure," said John. "The son was taken on board because he'd already earned your respect and proven himself through his actions. I mean, who wouldn't want someone like that working in their company?"

"Exactly! You can't buy that kind of loyalty, John. That's why I don't hesitate to clean up a few scraps of paper, because it helps my staff—my family."

"Why do you call your staff *family*, Mr. Cams?"

"My wife and I didn't start this company, young man. My father, who inherited it from his father, handed it down to me. We have always been a family-run business. I chose to continue with that mindset. While we might not be related, we are family operated.

"So you get to *choose* your family," said John. "Boy, it would be nice if we all could choose our family members. I know for sure that everyone in *my* family would choose to enjoy Thanksgiving dinner without my tipsy Uncle Paul."

The two chuckled. "Even though we can't choose our own family, John, we *can* choose who we associate with," continued the wise Mr. Cams.

"Someone once said we are an accumulation of the five people we associate with most—and our income is the average of those same five people.

"Ponder this—when you were in high school, if you hung out with kids who smoked, who were you?"

"A smoker, I suppose," John muttered.

"And if you hung around with the athletes? The math whizzes? How about the chess club people?"

"I understand," said John.

"So," Mr. Cams continued, "I did some serious soul searching on that notion, and it came to me like a bolt of lightning: *From this day forward, I will <u>choose</u> the company I keep.* At that moment, Mrs. Cams and I began our quest to surround ourselves with people who share our values. Let's see now where did I see that?" joked Mr. Cams as he stood next to a framed poster that adorned the hallway, rolling his eyes in its direction.

"Interesting," John replied as he wondered how he'd missed the movie-size poster. "Now, here's the best part," added Mr. Cams. "Once we started surrounding ourselves with the best people with the best intentions, we started receiving the best in return, for water seeks its own level. We chose to raise that level and —voila—we created our own family environment with like-minded members."

"I see. But, sir, how can you be sure that everyone is like-minded and shares your same level of enthusiasm about things?"

"I'm glad you asked. You see, I developed a plan," replied Mr. Cams. "I discovered the secret of like-thinking in my youth. My father was my role model, hero, and mentor all rolled into one. I loved and respected him, but we didn't always think alike.

"My father was incredibly wise, though, John. He knew young people have their own ideas, and you can't force your philosophies on them. Instead, he started me on an incentive reading program. Let's just say he knew my hot button, so he pressed it and made me an offer I couldn't refuse.

"He would select inspirational classics that emphasized attitude, loyalty, integrity, stewardship, responsibility, and accountability. He fed me short biographies of great leaders and devotional classics. He explained to me that biographies challenge the mind and devotionals speak to your heart.

"My incentive? I was rewarded financially for the quality of my book reviews.

"I found that I loved biographies, John. The principles they lived by are as important today as they were back then. I also could see a little of myself in each book and each life.

"Did you like the devotionals?" John inquired.

"At first, I didn't have much interest in the devotionals—that is, until my father shared one of his favorite quotes, which is still fresh in my mind today:

> *You can be born with ability,*
> *you can acquire knowledge, you can develop skill,*
> *but wisdom comes only from God.*

"One of my father's heroes was Abraham Lincoln. One of his favorite Lincoln quotes hung on a plaque on his office wall. It said, 'My best friend is a person who will give me a book I have not read.'

"The more I read, the more I began to think. I realized my father wasn't trying to get me to think like him, John, but to think the great thoughts that make all great leaders great."

"But how does this relate to your employees, or your family, as you call them?" John asked.

"When I was given the reins to lead the company, the idea my father used on me seemed to be the ideal way to create like-thinking people. We began the Book of the Month 'Reading-Thinking-Sharing' program. Here's how it works: everyone receives a free book selected by our review committee. They meet during lunch monthly in groups of six to eight people to discuss their book and share ideas, and then they receive another new book."

"What is the importance of the book club, and how can it really help anyone grow?" John wanted to know.

"One of my favorite quotes of all time comes from a most insightful truth and wisdom—'We are the same today as we will be in five years, besides the books we read and the people we meet.' To change one's life, simply take note of what we put into our minds and the people we share the information with."

John repeated the message aloud, mostly to himself. "We are the same today as we will be in five years, besides the books we read and the people we meet."

Mr. Cams leaned in, threw John a wink, and whispered, "Yes, son, and I've seen the people you associate with, so you better get reading!"

The young VP broke out into a grin and nodded. He got the message.

"I can't begin to tell you what this simple program has done to create like-thinking people in our company. It has impacted our people and their families. I'd like to share two letters, John, that I received recently as proof of the miracle power in reading together."

Pulling them out of his pocket, Mr. Cams read them out loud.

Dear Mr. Cams,

I must tell you what our book program has done for my family. I share our book club books with my father. These books mean so much to him and have built a great bond between us. His favorite book was "The Generosity Factor" by Ken Blanchard. He wept as he told me that this book finally gave purpose to his life. Thank you for this program.

Sincerely, Betty

Dear Mr. Cams,

I want to tell you what a difference the monthly reading program has made in my life. When I started working almost four years ago, I joined the book club right away because I felt it would help me get to know people. What I didn't know was how much the books I read were going to change my life.

I had spent 33 years with another industry and had become very mistrustful. I felt everyone was trying to stab me in the back. I still had that chip on my shoulder when I started working here. Within a couple of months reading the books, my whole attitude changed. I even got a letter from my younger sister saying how nice it was to have her sister back. My attitude is positive and hopeful today, and my life is so incredibly different than it used to be. Thank you! Thank you! Thank you!

Mary

"Now I ask you, is there any other program that could have done this so simply?

"We also use books to select like-thinking people in our employee interviews. We found a very special book, *The Ultimate Gift,* that presents very clearly the values of our company. We ask prospective employees to read it before their final interview. Here is a letter from a prospective employee:"

Dear Mr. Cams,

I sat down last night to read what I thought would be a few chapters of The Ultimate Gift and ended up finishing the book. I can't thank you enough. This impacted my life. I have finally come to realize what my father has been trying to teach me for years. I couldn't understand why I had to have a job at 15 years old and why my parents did not help me out when I did not work, but gave me many gifts when I was working. I now understand that my father is not as petty as I thought; he worked hard for everything that he has in life, and he appreciates it. I learned that success is achieved through hard work, and I hold the key to that success in my hands. I have come to realize that I am young, I have my whole life ahead of me, and I have to pay my dues, just like everyone else in the business world has done. Success is not given; it is earned.

Thank you again for giving me the opportunity to read this book. I am now on the right path to begin my first career. I understand that it will take time, hard work, and dedication to get to the level I dream of one day, but I can get there as long as I put in the effort.

I have developed a new appreciation for my life, my family, and my belongings.

Sincerely, Sally

"Naturally, we hired Sally and her like-thinking helped in our decision. I've found there are many ingredients in building a great team. I'm convinced that like-thinking people are our greatest asset and our Read-Think-Share program has been our best investment."

"Thank you for sharing this with me," John said. "I can clearly see the value of what you are doing. It is so simple." Then, shaking his head, he added, "It's amazing how difficult it is to see the obvious."

"We truly care about each other like family, John. If someone's out sick, it's not uncommon for someone else to work extra hours to do their work. If someone needs help sending their kids to college, we have a program to assist them with that. And if—"

"Someone sees a piece of paper on the floor, they pick it up to help someone else out," John interrupted, finishing his mentor's sentence.

Mr. Cams paused to flash a bright smile and give his pupil a nod in agreement. "You know something, young man? At this rate, you may just 'get it,' after all."

John smiled in return as Mr. Cams whispered, "Pssssst—here's the secret. You know they say to treat people like *you* want to be treated?"

"Yes," replied John.

"It's a lie," attested the mentor.

As he'd done a few times in the past couple days, John was once again puzzled, wondering what was coming next.

"Treat people the way *they* want to be treated. You see, we all have different ideas, dreams, and desires. Find out what those things are for each person and talk to them about their interests," Mr. Cams said, tossing his arm across his new friend's shoulders.

Then, turning John toward the door that leads into the factory, the mentor whispered these final words into John's ear, "The more you know about people, the easier it is to treat them as they want to be treated. You'll also create friends and alliances, and you'll gain respect. Now, let's go meet the family."

be a star

As the two men pushed through the large swinging doors leading into the factory, John couldn't help but notice the giant monitor that greeted them. Stars of every size and color flashed on and off the screen, creating the opening act for the message that was its main attraction:

BE A STAR!

Though it would have been hard to miss, he took a moment to

silently congratulate himself for noticing the screen without someone having to call his attention to it. Then his attention was drawn to the people bustling around the floor, yet none of the machinery was moving. It appeared that they were getting ready to close down the shop for an extended time—like they were preparing for a long vacation or something.

"What's going on?" he asked.

"Spring cleaning," answered Mr. Cams. "I'm glad you came today to see how we keep things *new* within these old walls."

"You've got that right," agreed John. "This place looks immaculate. I've never seen a factory so clean and well organized before. What's the secret?"

Mr. Cams led the way to an area perched above the factory floor. Pointing down toward the middle of the work area, he explained, "Well, it's simple, really—not rocket science or some crazy new idea—and we're so used to it, we hardly think about it anymore."

"So, what is it?" the young entrepreneur asked, anxious for an answer.

"We switch," replied the mentor.

"Switch? I don't understand."

"You see, every six months to a year, we switch our general labor positions. That way, we get our family cross-trained in every job here," he informed John.

"Doesn't that scare the employees? Aren't they afraid they may lose their job security?"

"Well, let me ask you something. Who would be more valuable at your company—someone who knows how to do *one* thing, or someone who knows how to do *everything?* I compare it to having a paring knife or a Swiss Army knife—you know, one with all the bells and whistles. If you were out in the woods, which one would have more value?"

Even though the look on the young man's face showed his agreement, he had a frightening vision of the mass hysteria such a bold move would cause within his corporation.

"Now, I know what you're thinking," interjected Mr. Cams, "and to be honest, I thought the same thing when someone first suggested this idea to me many years ago. You think people are going to jump ship, right?"

John acknowledged his statement with a nod of the head, while the look on his face said, *How did he know what I was thinking?*

The older gentleman continued. "To be honest, a few of our employees did jump ship when we first started this switching thing. But as I said, it's become such a habit now that no one thinks twice about it anymore. As for the newer employees, this is all they know. And to be honest, we all now look forward to switching day.

"Have you ever had a job and wished you could do something different or switch with someone else in the company? Well, this is their opportunity to do just that. The best thing, believe it or not, is that each new person adds his or her own twist to the fresh assignment. By the simple laws of evolution, the position eventually streamlines itself. The way a job is done now—let alone a year ago or five years ago—is more productive and efficient than ever before."

"I'm curious—who suggested this to you?" inquired John. "A vice-president? An auditing firm?"

"You'd think so, but actually it came from one of our three-star suggestions," replied the teacher.

"Your three-star what?"

"Let me explain, John. You see, on our company's anniversary, during our annual potluck dinner, each employee can submit three suggestions that he or she feels would improve the company. The suggestions can pertain to any of the departments because, after all, we 'switch' departments. Then we implement the best ideas. If we use an idea of yours, for example, you receive a thousand dollars in cash, a plaque is presented to you in front of all of your peers, and your name is engraved on the Walk of Fame. Do you see the Walk of Fame down there?"

Mr. Cams pointed to the floor leading into what appeared to be the lunchroom. John noticed that the entire area was decorated in the same movie theater style he saw in his mentor's office, with stars on the ground like those on Hollywood Boulevard and Vine. While he couldn't make out the writing, he could see that each star was inscribed with an employee's name.

"Holy smokes! That's a great idea," he exclaimed. "They must love it."

"Yes, we all do," agrees Mr. Cams, "and it's consistent with our movie motif. I think it's a nice personal touch that encourages employee engagement, as your generation refers to it, and it provides an incentive for feedback and interaction."

"So, what you have here," John observed, "is a company full of cross-trained, happy, motivated, family-oriented people all working together to create success."

"That's right, and we have *fun* doing it, too," replied the mentor. "It's a bit like a great little book I picked up a while back. Maybe you've heard of it; it's called *Fish!—A Remarkable Way to Boost Morale and Improve Results,* and it was co-authored by Stephen C. Lundin and my friend, Harry Paul. It's an amazing story of how these guys took a smelly job like selling fish at Pike Place Market in Seattle and turned it into a world-famous tourist attraction. And they had a ball doing it."

"How so?" John asked, keenly interested.

"They took what most would view as a horrible work environment and turned it into one of the most enjoyable, positive, and energetic places to work in America. They made the best of their conditions by having fun. Who knew selling fish could be fun, right? Well, they found a way. They put on a performance and figured out how to make selling fish entertaining! They threw the fish across the room, behind their backs, and over their customers' heads, and they even put their hands inside them, like puppets, so they could move their mouths and make them look like they were talking. I'm telling you, it's quite a show—and at the end of the day, they sell *huge* amounts of product while having the time of their lives. People come from across the globe to watch these guys at work.

"The moral of the story, I thought to myself, is that if these guys could make the most of what they had to work with, just imagine what insurance agencies, real estate offices, accounting firms, and all other businesses could do. John, it reminds me of that old saying: *When you love your work, you'll never work a day in your life."*

"How did you use this concept for your place?"

"We made work fun, just like you've seen, by creating the movie theater theme and the Walk of Fame, and establishing ongoing contests," replied the mentor.

"You have contests, too?"

"Yep. One of the best parts of working here is that we're always running new contests. The employees come up with fun, innovative ways to help increase morale and revenue at the same time. For example, last month, we held a Lobster Feast."

"Say what?" asked John.

"We went to a party supply store and found plastic lobsters, starfish, and other sea doodads, and we hung them all over the place—from the ceilings, on the walls and doors—wherever! Then, when production went up by our projected goal of 12 percent (which had never been done before, by the way), we had a lobster feast. We flew in a boatload of live Maine lobsters and cooked them up out there in the parking lot. The family pitched in and set up tables and chairs outside, and everyone contributed to the rest of the fixins', and before we knew it, we were having a crustacean extravaganza! That was a blast. Everyone's still talking about it.

"From that big push by our team, revenues increased and profits more than covered the cost of the feast. And even better, we're on track to do it again this month, because now everyone knows it's possible—the momentum is there for ongoing profit."

"That's just incredible," exclaimed John. Then he asked his next question with sincere interest, "Do all of the contests include an expensive payout?"

"Oh, absolutely not," assured the mentor. "In fact, one of the best ones we ever did, and had a blast doing, was called *Boss for the Day*. It didn't cost a dime."

"What did you do?" asked the engaged student.

"For one full week, in each department, whoever produced the highest volume with the fewest errors got to be Boss for the Day the following Monday.

"Whoever won in their division would show up at the factory (if they chose to) in a suit or nice outfit, instead of their work smock, and they got to sit in the boss's office, enjoy a cup of coffee, and act as the manager for the entire day—while the supervisor worked the winner's position in return. It was great! Now, we're doing it all the time," bragged the proud adviser, "because we began to see that some employees can rise up to take on a managerial role, and it keeps the supervisor in touch with the staff at the same time."

"Talk about a freebie and a win-win proposition," exclaimed the young Mr. Bishop.

The mentor smiled at his impressed protégé. Then he put his arm around John's shoulders and led him down a flight of stairs toward the middle of the workplace.

"Let me introduce you to somebody. Maria, come over here for a second, please?" announced Mr. Cams. "John, this is my right-hand woman, Maria, or as we call her around here, the director," Mr. Cams clarified as he introduced his manager to the young guest.

"Hello. Nice to meet you," John smiled and reached out to shake Maria's hand. "Mr. Cams has been so kind to show me around your impressive organization and teach me some of your secrets."

Smiling warmly at the introduction, Maria replied, "It's great to meet you, as well. However, what you're learning is no secret. We want *everyone* to share this information and succeed in his or her own company. Let me ask you, do you think you could implement some of these ideas in your company?"

"Well," John pondered, "it's not that I think people would reject the ideas as much as I think that ..."

"So you *don't* think people will be receptive, do you?" interrupted Mr. Cams.

"That's not what I said," John protested.

"That's *exactly* what you said, young man," lectured the mentor as Maria continued to convey the message.

"You see, John, one of the things Mr. Cams teaches us is to listen to what people are *telling us*, rather than what they are *saying.*"

John tilted his head to one side, not quite understanding what he was hearing.

"It's like this," Maria explained. "After watching and studying human behavior, Mr. Cams noticed a few trends that changed the way we all look at and listen to others. He refers to them as his 99 percent rules. It's probably even closer to 100 percent, but our mentor here gives himself a little 'out' for those of us who want to find a loophole in his theory. We haven't found many loopholes, mind you, but we have discovered that looking for these common denominators in everyday conversation helps us to read between the lines quicker.

"After years of studying human interaction, Mr. Cams came up with a few 99 percent rules that really seem to work. First, when someone starts a sentence with 'It's not,' he's usually trying to tell you 'It is' without hurting your feelings. Second, when someone starts a sentence with 'I don't,' she's trying to tell you ' I do.'

"Here are some examples," she continued. "If a person says, 'It's not you, it's me,' he's struggling to tell you, 'It's you.' When he says, 'It's not that you are too short,' he's actually thinking you are too short.

Someone might say, 'It's not that I have a drinking problem,' but then goes on to tell a story about a time he drank too much. Get the picture?"

The wheels in John's mind spinning rapidly, he managed a nod as he attempted to take it all in.

"You see, John," added Mr. Cams, "when I interrupted you a minute ago, it was because you said, 'It's *not* that I think people would reject the idea.' Using my 99 percent rule, I knew you were telling me that you thought people *would* reject the idea."

"Here's how I use the 99 percent rule every day to help me cut to the chase and find out what's really on someone's mind," added Maria. "Let's say that a salesperson comes into my office and begins a pitch with, 'It's not that we need the money, we're simply trying to help you gain a new product line for your corporation.' Now, whatever comes out of this person's mouth next doesn't really make a difference, because I know by using this rule that what he really wants is to raise capital. So I would stop him mid-sentence and say, 'Listen, you need money, and I could use your product. Forget the five dollars that you want for each unit. Let me save us both some time. I'll give you what you really want—cash! I can give you two dollars each. Do you want it?'

"You see, once you master listening to what people are actually telling you, it puts you in control and can save a lot of time and hassle in the long run," Maria concluded.

"I get it," nodded the younger man in excitement. "Now, what was the other rule you were talking about?"

"The other example I mentioned was the phrase, 'I don't,' as in 'I don't want to tell you,' In that case, she's usually trying to *direct you* without hurting your feelings. For example, 'I don't want to tell you how to raise your children, but—' or, 'I don't want to tell you how to drive, but—' or 'I don't want to tell you to take my side, but—'"

"That's great!" blurted out the young Mr. Bishop. "Absolutely great! I hear those words every day. It's kind of like the word *try* in my office."

The manager and her boss looked at John, puzzled. "Please continue," Mr. Cams urged.

"Well, you kept using the word *try* in your examples. They *try* not to hurt your feelings. As we all know, *try* means to fail or simply not do something. When you ask someone, 'Hey, are you going to the party tonight?' and they respond, 'I'll try,' that pretty much means no, right? So when I need something done around my office, I listen for that word and then run from it."

Maria and Mr. Cams chuckled a bit, nodding in agreement as John continued his explanation.

"It's like this. When I go up to someone and ask, 'Can you get this report on my desk by 9 A.M. tomorrow?' and they say, 'I'll try,' I simply take the document from them and ask someone else. If they too, say they'll try to get it done, I continue on my quest until I run into that one person who says, 'No problem.' That's the person who gets the job done."

"Excellent!" voiced Mr. Cams. "I think you've got it! It's like when someone says it's the *last* thing he wants to do, it usually becomes the *first* thing he actually does. Like when a person says, 'The last thing I want to do is hurt your feelings, but I'm breaking up with you,' or 'The last thing I want to do is tell you how to do your job.'"

"But—" John and Maria both spoke up in unison.

Laughing, Mr. Cams said, "Well, I think we've all learned a little something new today. John, why don't you roam around on your own for a bit and then join us in the theater for lunch in an hour?"

"The theater? That sounds great. I'll see you there. It's *not* that I'll be hungry by then."

Grinning at John's play on words, Mr. Cams and Maria left their guest to explore on his own.

mentoring your way
to million$

"This place is great!" boomed John as he walked into the lunchroom with a tone and stride so confident it was like he owned the place.

"Glad you think so," responded Maria. Then, noticing the three smiling faces at his side, she added, "It looks like you found some new friends."

"I sure did," said John. "This is Marcos, Sharon, and Hank."

"Yes, I know—they're family," Maria remarked.

"That's why they look familiar," teased Mr. Cams.

John grinned sheepishly as his cheeks reddened. "I feel like I've known these people for years," he said. "Great people and a great environment. This place is dynamite. I've learned more about high-quality manufacturing in this last hour than in my previous ten years."

"What did you learn?" asked Sharon as she turned to face their visitor.

"Well, I learned, first and foremost, that there are no such things as *secrets.*"

The whole group cringed slightly and waited for him to elaborate.

"Let me explain," John continued. "For years, I thought many of the things I was doing were my original thoughts and ideas. I swore everyone to secrecy about my great 'trade secrets' to success and even kept many thoughts to myself so no one would steal them. Then I come here and take a quick walk through your plant and find that not only are my so-called secrets not so secret, but everyone here is doing them better than me."

Mr. Cams and his family laughed.

"Everyone I talked to today shared their thoughts with me openly. Each one knows what the other one is doing. And they all help one another; notice I didn't say—*try* to help one another. I'm definitely impressed. I've never seen a company operate so smoothly. It's remarkable. Like I said, this place is dynamite."

"You make a good point," agreed Marcos. "I never thought about it before because this is the only way I know. I was hired right out of school; this was my first job, and to this day, it's the only job I've ever had. I thought *every* company ran this way. I mean, why would you keep secrets and keep your *own* people in the dark?"

The group quickly turned to John for an answer, their faces asking the unspoken question, *Yeah, why would you have secrets?*

John chuckled and said, "I bet every organization in the world thinks they have the greatest ideas and no one else knows them. While the administration keeps sales in the dark, the sales staff hides stuff from accounting, and the shipping department is the last to know anything. The only person who knows everything is the receptionist at the front desk. Meanwhile, some little shop in Kansas is probably doing the exact same thing, only more efficiently and never knowing it's some 'great wisdom' somewhere else."

The lights in the lunchroom suddenly went dim, and Mr. Cams turned to John and whispered, "Well, it looks like it's show time. Let's move along while the family enjoys their break. I want to show you something."

As people scrambled for their seats, a large screen dropped down from the ceiling, and a familiar face popped up and began speaking.

"Isn't that Zig Ziglar, the author and motivational speaker?" John asked, turning his head back to the screen as he and his host exited the theater toward their next quest.

"Sure is," replied the mentor. "Once a week, we play inspirational messages on the big screen for the family. The other days, they usually watch TV or play games during their break."

"Unbelievable," John whispered, shaking his head.

"What's so unbelievable about that?"

"What if they get so inspired that they leave and open their own company?" he asked.

"That would be *great*," Mr. Cams replied.

"What?" shrieked John.

"I said, that would be great," repeated the adviser. "Let me give you an example. I call it mentoring your way to millions. It's a powerful message and, in today's business environment, I believe it's time to dust it off and share it with others once more.

"You've heard it time and time again from our man, Zig: *To get what you want out of life, you must first help others get what they want.* Reacquainting yourself with this principle is not only a good way to live, it's a great way to do business.

"Over the years, I've watched many start-up companies come and go. Their failures and setbacks got me wondering what happened. Where did they go wrong? But then I began to ask a bigger question, rephrased in a more positive manner—What did all the *successful* businesses do right? The answer is right there in the first thing I said, summarized like this:

"The more you mentor others, share what you know, learn, and earn, the more you solidify your chances to succeed at any endeavor. Commit to mentoring, and you can literally mentor your way to millions!

"Say you run a business—large or small. If it's your true desire to help everyone succeed, from the receptionist to you as the CEO, guess what? You will. Just help others get what *they* want first, and your own success will soon follow.

"Okay, right now you're probably asking yourself, 'How can I do that?'"

"You've got that right," John agreed.

"It's simple, really. The first thing you need to do is find out what motivates the people around you and commit to helping them achieve it. The second thing is to know who really counts in the company. Over the years, if there's *one* thing I've learned, it's that two of the most important positions in any organization are the receptionists and sales executives."

"Why?" asked John.

"They're the people who interact most with your customers, and they're the people with the greatest potential to create new customers," answered Mr. Cams. "Happy receptionists and loyal, motivated sales reps are ambassadors for your company's positive image.

"Let's take that receptionist you were talking about earlier to illustrate how easily mentoring your way to millions can work—and work it does! Let's say your receptionist wants to go back to school to study nursing. We'll call her Nancy—we won't use my wife for this example, because you'd probably just be rude to her," teased Mr. Cams as John cringed. "Nancy tells you about her goal during the one-on-one orientation meeting you have with every new staff member, the meeting where you ask, 'If you could choose any career for yourself, what would you choose?'

"Once she's shared her goal with you, you congratulate her on a great choice of career paths and tell her why you're going to help make her dream a reality. Now, Nancy is no fool. Of course not—you don't hire fools because 'We are the company we keep.' Remember?"

John nodded as he knowingly smiled.

"She may even ask why you'd support her in something that will eventually cause her to leave your organization—just as you're wondering right now. You tell her, 'Nancy, you are a valuable employee, and I'll be sorry to see you go one day, but I realize that by helping you achieve your true goal in life, you will be happier.

And happy people make great employees.' Cheerful and content, she'll give you 100 percent and earnestly train someone to replace herself when she moves on to her new career."

Mr. Cams continued, "Just imagine Nancy's excitement when, a few days later, you show a genuine interest in her goal by giving her a variety of brochures from local nursing academies—brochures you requested on her behalf. You tell her she can take a few minutes each day on the company phone to contact the schools and set up a class schedule that works for her.

"Now, here's where the true mentoring comes in. You take a moment to share with her your experiences with change. You reflect on how *you* felt and the fears *you* faced when you gave up your job to start at the company she works for now. You detail how you overcame obstacles and shut out the noise of the naysayers who told you all the reasons your idea was crazy and why you should forget about it. You let her know you're there to act as a positive support, a constant reminder that she can achieve her dream. You reinforce the message that if and when she needs guidance, encouragement, or a shoulder to lean on during her transition, she can count on you.

"Consider how great Nancy will feel walking into the office each day knowing that, at the end of regular business hours, she'll be heading right toward her life's goal—to become a nurse and help others. How will she answer your company phone from that day forward? What do you suppose her tone of voice and enthusiasm level will be when someone asks her about the place where she works?"

"Wow," John reflected, "I can just imagine what a terrific first impression she'll make on potential customers and job applicants who walk through the front door every day!"

"It paints a really pretty picture, doesn't it?"

"It sure does," replied the eager student.

"Mentoring your way to millions is a win-win proposition," Mr. Cams continued. "Let's face it, the more you help others identify and pursue their dreams, the greater support and backing you get from them in return. It just makes sense! No one wants to be just a cog in the system, a faceless wage slave, day in and day out for the rest of their lives.

"When you show your people that you recognize their worth, and you support not only their goals in the workplace but their hopes and dreams outside the system, they'll do amazing things. They'll rise above adversity and give their all to you and your business. Why? Because you've given them something all too rare in life—unconditional support. After all, they're family.

"Step back and imagine, if you will, your company filled with people who feel important and appreciated—people who actually *want* to come to work each day. What if *your* job became making the round and checking that everyone was keeping up with their life goals, as well as their job assignments? Guess what? It can happen! Just look up there," Mr. Cams suggested as he pointed to another large banner on the wall. It read:

The Greatest Success We'll Know is Helping Others Succeed and Grow

Like a light bulb going on, John abruptly shouted, "By George, I think I've got it!" as the two men strode purposefully out of the factory and burst through another set of gigantic doors.

a positive attitude
gets results

"What's down here?" the apprentice asked as the two men headed down the hallway.

"The past, the present, and the future," was the mentor's matter-of-fact response.

"Okay, Charles Dickens. Is this the part where you start reciting lines from *A Christmas Carol?*" John joked.

Letting out a belly laugh, Mr. Cams said, "You'd think so, with a setup like that, but I'm just going to take you into our Wall of Fame room. But I do admire that your mindset is in line with our theme."

The comment sparked John's curiosity.

"Hey, speaking of movies, what made you decide to decorate your factory with that theme?"

"Well, among other things, as you know, our company supplies movie projectors, posters, and wall decorations for movie houses — just like we did for your grandfather years back. And since we've become successful by taking action while chasing a dream, we put it all together and get 'Lights, Camera, Action!' The decorating theme seemed fitting, even obvious. Considering the fact that we sell this great stuff, we might as well use it ourselves, too. Don't you agree?"

The two came to a doorway adorned with similar red velvet theater curtains as those John noticed framing his mentor's office window during their first meeting.

"Ta-da," proclaimed Mr. Cams as they entered the room.

John is flabbergasted at the gallery of photos that wallpapered the entire room.

"This is what we call our Wall of Fame," explained Mr. Cams. "However, as you can see, it's really grown into our *room* of fame because we've almost run out of empty wall space.

"This wall shows the way the company looked under my father's care, and this wall shows what it looked like before him. This area shows all the family members under my regime, and the empty little spot in this corner is saved for the next group after me."

"This is awesome, Mr. Cams. I'm astounded. How do you keep coming up with this stuff?"

"Again, I'd like to take the credit, but it was my mother who collected all the photos. After someone came up with the whole Wall of Fame idea, I started tacking up the pictures so everyone could see where we came from and where we're going."

"What's this?" John asked, pointing to a diagram posted on a section of the wall.

"It's the future," answered Mr. Cams, "You might call it the bigger picture. It's what we believe is the company's destiny. The missus and I will probably just be spectators through that transition, watching someone else's passion catch fire. We've had a great run here, but when the time comes, we'll know. It's best to know when enough is enough, and simply let the new generation take over, as my father did before me, and his before him, and so on. But let's go. There's something else I want to show you."

Matching strides, the two headed out of the room. While earlier in the day, it had been difficult keeping up with his mentor, John now mirrored his quick pace to perfection.

Nearing the main office where they'd met the day before, they turned a corner. Before the mentor could speak, John saw a small replica of a marquee hanging over a doorway that read:

A Positive Attitude Will Not Get the Desired Result Every Time, but a Negative One Surely Will

"Great quote. Who said it?"

"My good friend, Anon."

"Anon?" John asked.

"Yes, you might know him yourself. Anon Ymous," Mr. Cams declared with a quick grin. "I'm sure some great philosopher said it first, but I don't know who to give the credit to."

Laughing, John thought to himself, *This guy is quite the card—he knows how to put fun into just about anything.*

"I'll tell you a quick story about this message," the older man began, when suddenly Ellen Cams appeared out of nowhere and cheerfully interjected, "No, let me tell it. This poor boy is probably tired of hearing you ramble on all day."

"Well, actually ..."

But John's attempt to deny her statement was cut short.

"Hush up, now," insisted Mrs. Cams. "It's *my* turn to talk."

The two gentlemen exchanged a grin and an *it-looks-like-she-told-us* look as Ellen launched into the story.

"You see, my husband is an avid tennis player—not a great one, but an avid one," she said, winking at Mr. Cams. "Well, someone made a comment to him on the tennis court one time that really got him thinking. This person was a much more talented player, and he was beating Oscar to a pulp. Oscar piped up in his usual manner, 'Here I come. Watch out now; here comes my 'A' game. I have you right where I want you. Listen! I can hear the theme from *Rocky* in the background.'"

Mr. Cams broke his silence and chimed in. "It was no big deal—just the usual pep talk, right? The funny thing is that I actually *believed* I could pull out a win if I just kept focusing on enjoying the game and playing my best. However, it was how my opponent responded that really got me thinking. He said, 'You know, it's great that you have such a positive attitude and everything, but that's not going to win you games.'

"Wow, what a statement, I thought to myself, and I suddenly had a realization. I rushed home afterward to write it down and that's what you see up here on this marquee. *A positive attitude will not get the desired result every time; however, a negative one surely will."*

"Mr. Cams did win that tennis match, by the way," Mrs. Cams added with a smile. Then, without missing a beat, she continued the dialogue as if she and her husband had rehearsed this routine a dozen times before. "You see, every successful individual we know, past or present, has *one* true common variable we can think of: *Successful people all have an overly zealous positive attitude and clearly believe they will ultimately succeed.* Think of all the great American icons who shared the same characteristics. Imagine such people as Henry Ford, Steve Jobs, and the Wright brothers."

John added, "Thomas Edison, Bill Gates, and Abraham Lincoln."

"Yes!" she congratulated. "Can you imagine any of them saying something like, 'This is too hard, I'm way out of my league, or let's just forget about it'?"

Mr. Cams boomed in, "Of course not! They kept pushing on through all their adversities and setbacks, believing they'd eventually succeed as long as they kept believing in the beauty of their dream."

"That reminds me of what my old coach used to tell me," said John. "Quitters never win, and winners never quit."

"So, now I put this same scenario to you," Mr. Cams said in a game-show-host tone. "What would you do, right now, if you believed that you, too, couldn't fail? Would you ask that person you've had a crush on out on a date? What about taking action on that crazy idea or invention that you've simply been putting off until the right time? Would you write a book? Adopt a child? Start a new business? Challenge a better player in tennis?" Waving his arms in excitement, Mr. Cams looked the younger businessman in the eye and once again asked, "What would you do? What could you do?"

Mrs. Cams calmed the moment, bringing it down a notch. "When you think about it, we all have wonderful things running through our minds from time to time. We get all excited about an idea, but then what happens? We let stinkin' thinkin' set in—that's what! We talk ourselves into believing it's never going to work, the challenge is *too* great, or that special someone won't like us because of the car we drive. What if they say no? What if our idea doesn't work? What if no one reads our book? In other words—"

"We give ourselves reasons to fail," John jumped in.

"Or even worse— reasons to *never* take a chance or put our dreams into action in the first place," Mrs. Cams said, finishing the thought in tag-team fashion.

As she paused to take a breath, her husband kept the dialogue going. "Here's a *big* newsflash. Assuming we don't already have a special someone, a book, or an idea in motion, *what do we have to lose?* However, by taking the first step and believing in ourselves, our dreams, and our desires, while maintaining a positive attitude toward the outcome, we can only move in one direction."

"Forward!" John exclaimed. "It reminds me of a friend of mine. A week or so ago, we were having lunch together at a restaurant. We spotted this beautiful woman there, and my friend mentioned that he'd love to go out with her. I suggested that he go over and ask her out on a date, but he replied, 'What if she says no?' I said, 'She's already *not* going out with you, so you have nothing to lose here. In reality, you can only gain a date.'"

"So, no matter what, he *can't* fail," said Mr. Cams. "The worst thing that can happen is your friend doesn't go out with her. Like you said, he's already doing that!"

"Right!" John responded. "I really like this one. It makes sense and gets me thinking."

"If you like that, let's finish our day by stopping by my office. I'll show you something that changed *my* life," offered the older gentleman.

Realizing that an irresistible offer had just presented itself, John agreed. Bidding a temporary farewell to Mrs. Cams, the two companions headed toward the big oak doors leading back to the main entrance.

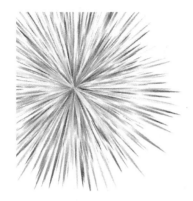

it doesn't matter
who gets the credit

As the two gentlemen reentered the host's unique office, John was the first to speak. "Wait a second," he grinned. "I don't see anything. Isn't there a flashing sign or a banner for this lesson?"

"Not for this one," the mentor replied.

Being melodramatic, the young entrepreneur clutched his chest as if in shock.

"But I do have a plaque," the mentor smiled, pointing to a wooden carving on his desk. "I saw this years ago on Ronald Reagan's desk in the Oval Office, and it changed my view of things—especially business—in a wonderful way."

Young John read it aloud:

"There is no limit to what a man can do so long as he does not care a straw who gets the credit for it." - Charles Edward Montague

"Do you remember, John, when you first came into my office, and I told you that I was a lot like you in my past?"

The pupil nodded—he remembered it well.

"Well, here's what I meant by that. You see, you came barging into this building with so much arrogance that it would be intimidating to most, yet with an enthusiasm that keeps people around. Everyone wants to back a winning team, young man, but few will stay after the victory if they're not appreciated for their contributions."

After slumping his head into his chest for a moment, John met the older man's eyes. His words and his tone both humble, he responded, "I get it. All this time I was bragging about my own accomplishments, telling everyone how great I was in creating success in my life when, after all, it was those around me who actually did the work. I just took the credit for it."

"Excellent!" Mr. Cams applauded with a clap of his hands.

"It is?"

"Yes. Of all the things you've learned, this is the most important: *We are only as good as the company we keep.*"

John signified his understanding with a nod of the head. "So, Mr. Cams, it's like you said before—to be truly successful, surround yourself with only the best people you can find, treat them like family, help them attain their goals through mentorship, and let them share in the success."

"Sounds pretty nice, doesn't it?" a voice from behind him asked.

John turned his head to find a much older man in a wheelchair at the door.

"You must be Mr. Bishop, the chosen one I've been hearing so much about. Let me introduce myself. My name is Mr. Cams—senior, that is. The same message that you just recited, I learned from my father, then I shared it with the young whippersnapper before you, my son, Oscar Cams, Jr."

John looked at his host with a warm smile and an expression of disbelief at the thought of his mentor still being a child in someone's eyes. "I'm sorry," he said uncertainly, returning his attention to the man in the doorway. "Did you say the *chosen* one?"

"Sure did. You don't think you're standing here for nothing, do you? Listen, I know you've had a long day, so this will be the final story a Cams will share with you today. Let me assure you right now that, yes, you *are* the chosen one. In fact, we are *all* the chosen ones.

"Think about it. Right now, I'm sure there's something you're an expert in, something you have a true passion for, perhaps it's a sport you play, the company you run, your community involvement, or simply finding great fulfillment in the family you hold together. When all is said and done, haven't we all pondered the age-old question: *What is the meaning of life?* Well, perhaps it's not so much the meaning of life itself that's so puzzling, but the more personal question of: *What's my purpose?* And *What's the meaning of my life?*

"I believe we were put on Earth for a purpose, young man, and it's our job to find out what that purpose is. Then, even more important, we need to fulfill that calling by taking action on it."

As his wise father stopped to gather his thoughts, Cams Jr. continued, "Have you ever wondered how and why Greenpeace activists throw themselves in front of freightliners? Or why firefighters rush into places others are escaping and running away from? Or why some executives or inventors spend their whole lives in pursuit of the one thing that drives them? That is their passion. It is their purpose. And in pursuing that passion, these people are separated from the masses by just one thing—they're living the life they love."

"Wow," John said in amazement. "Perhaps the reason I've hit the glass ceiling, as I told you when we first met, is because I've always looked at my business as a business, rather than as something I live to do."

"Do you want to know the secret to ultimate fulfillment?" Mr. Cams, Sr. asked.

"Of course," replied the eager student.

"Find out what that purpose is for you, and then pursue it with everything you have. Then you'll never be worried about what positions people hold in your company, or you won't care that you may have to take one step back to go twenty steps forward. All those things won't matter, because each day you'll be living the life you love, the life you've chosen, rather than one that has chosen you."

Like a light bulb turned on in his head, John raised his index finger in emphasis at his new discovery. "And *that's* why you don't worry about switching positions here, or who gets the credit, or even if they wish to do something else one day, because you're focused on what you love!"

As he finished voicing his revelation, an idea hit him from out of nowhere, and he said to his new friends, "Thank you so much for your time today. Words cannot express how much I appreciate your help."

"You're right," Mr. Cams, Sr. firmly agreed. *"Words* cannot express it. Show us how much you appreciate the advice by simply applying it."

The young man stopped in his tracks and with all the sincerity he could muster, said, "Yes, sir, I will."

"Before you go," Mr. Cams, Sr. continued, "let me end our conversation here by sharing this last thought with you. One of the greatest secrets to truly living a balanced and fruitful life is to remember to practice what you preach, because someone is always watching."

"They are?" John asked.

"Yes, they are. Remember, in some form, in some way, to somebody, while you're on this big spinning rock we call Earth, whether you signed up for it or not, no matter how large or small, you're going to make an impact on someone else's life. We all have a special gift to share with the world. We all are the chosen ones, so we owe it to ourselves and everyone to find out what our special gift is and make an impact by pursuing it."

"And since this is true," interrupted the younger Cams, finishing his father's message, "the impact we make should be a positive one. In other words, shouldn't we all do our very best to make a positive impact?"

John acknowledged the two wise gentlemen by humbly nodding his head in agreement and whispering, "Absolutely," like he'd just been given the secrets of the universe.

As he prepared to leave, John reached out to shake their hands, but Mr. Cams, Jr. walked around his desk to send him off with one of his usual bear hugs. This time, John wasn't surprised. Instead of being shocked at the gesture, he hugged the two men back. As he walked out the door, he turned back to wave at them one more time before heading for home.

wake up and
live the life you love

In the parking structure, John approached his bright red Ferrari, sitting where he'd left it such a short time ago. Glancing at the rear window, he read the sticker that he'd placed there: "He who dies with the most toys wins."

Suddenly realizing how foolish he'd been, John reached into his pocket and pulled out his Platinum Visa card and used it to scrape under the decal, trying to remove it as quickly as he could.

There's an old saying that goes: *Many receive good advice, but few actually profit from it.* John was the exception to this rule. He has one talent that makes him shine above the rest. You see, John was smart enough to make the appointment to meet his new mentor, and then, even more important, he was smart enough to realize he needed to follow the great advice he'd just been given.

As John climbed behind the wheel and started the engine, he chuckled to himself, realizing how childish his behavior had been. He'd been arrogant, with an inflated, self-righteous attitude, believing the world owed him everything, while he owed little in return. He felt like a giant mirror had been placed before him, and he finally knew how others had been seeing him for a long time. This sudden "reflection" reminded him of a quote in a movie he once saw: *We all need mirrors to remind us who we are.*

The next morning, John entered his company as he's done for years — only this time he noticed some differences. Or perhaps they weren't really differences at all. Perhaps, he was finally seeing them for the first time.

As the receptionist behind the front desk tried to juggle all the phone calls that appeared to be overwhelming her, he noticed a panicked look on her face, as though she wished for nothing more than a moment of peace and a chance to catch her breath.

He entered the elevator, where three coworkers were already on board. As they all rode together to their perspective floors, John became aware, for the first time, that none of them had spoken to him or even acknowledged that he was there. They rode in silence, staring at the flashing numbers as the floors passed by.

Reaching the grand entrance to his office, he noticed that the doors were closed. As he drew near, his assistant simply said, "Your messages, sir." At that moment, John realized she'd been with him for over three years, and he didn't know anything about her — he had no idea where she lived, or even the names of her three children, whose photos were very obviously on display on her desk.

As John opened the doors to his workspace, a blast of musky odor emitting from his dark, overcrowded office made him step back. He noticed for the first time that the windows hadn't been opened in years, and the blinds, which had been drawn shut to keep out the sunlight, made the room seem dark and uninviting.

Why did I want a huge corner office with lots of windows, only to make sure I couldn't look out of them? Walking behind his oversized, solid mahogany desk with the huge nameplate to match, he sat in his executive leather chair, which was purposely raised on a perch (so he would always sit higher than anyone seated in the chair across from him). Still holding his car keys in his hand, he glanced at the Ferrari symbol and unhappily realized how others saw him. As he reflected on the comment made to Mr. Cams about *A Christmas Carol*, it occurred to him that people had to think he was totally self-centered, greedy, and maybe even mean. *They must think I'm totally unapproachable. They probably envision me as another Ebenezer Scrooge.*

Looking around his workspace, he realized how impersonal it was. There were no color photos of his family or of anything he loved in his life—only charts, memos, and Post-it notes to remind him of his next deadline. There was just one exception—tucked in the corner of the room was a faded black-and-white picture of John and his father standing in front of his grandpa's old theater, back when it was the pride of the town.

How did I even make it this far? John wondered to himself, shaking his head in self-disappointment as he lowered his forehead onto his palms.

At this moment, the change begins.

"Mary, can you come in here for a moment?" John called out to his trusted assistant.

As she walked into the room, he told her to put down the pencil and notepad that never left her side.

"We won't need these today," he said.

The look of shock on Mary's face spoke volumes. Perhaps her supervisor was ill; she knew something wasn't right. In the three years she'd been working for him, he had never once begun his day without boisterously dictating his schedule to the help.

"What can I do for you?" she asked as she took her customary seat across from her supervisor.

"The first thing you can do for me," began the new Mr. Bishop, "is to help me brighten this place up a bit. Let's open these blinds and windows, for gosh sakes, and let some light in. Oh, and if you would be so kind, I'd appreciate it if you would please order some plants for this office. And, even more important, order some flowers for your desk. Get a bright, cheery bouquet."

In disbelief, and amazement, Mary's jaw dropped ever so slightly.

John then asked her if she'd go shopping after lunch.

"I think we need some motivational posters, maybe a dozen or so. In the meantime, I'm going to check into getting some electronic signs. It might be a great way to make announcements and spread some positivity around here, don't you think?"

"Sure, Mr. Bishop," his assistant replied, trying to hide her puzzlement at the abrupt change in her supervisor's behavior.

What came next was a surprise to both of them. John said, "Before you do that, would you please do me a personal favor? I know it's not your job, but would you please go downstairs and help the receptionist answer phones? It seems she's overwhelmed and could use some assistance right now. In fact, if that's the case, kindly let me know so we can be sure to get her some permanent help right away."

Mary's face lit up at the proposition. "I'd be *very* happy to, sir."

"Mary, from now on, I'd like it if you call me J.B.," he said, leaving his assistant at a loss for words.

"You must be wondering what's come over me, and I'll explain later. What's important for you to know right now is that I've changed, and things around here are going to change for the better. I'd appreciate your help in developing a new environment. I want everyone to be happy to work here and proud to be part of this company."

"I'd be delighted to help you, sir—I mean J.B.," Mary replied with a smile.

After opening the windows and blinds and spraying some air freshener, Mary left to begin her assignment of making their workplace people friendly. John knew these were small changes, but they were a step toward the transformation he wanted to make. As the breeze blew through his sunlit office for the first time, it seemed as if it uplifted him and gave him a much-needed breath of fresh air— in more ways than one.

Days went by, turning into months, and, eventually, five years had passed. A little bit older and a lot wiser, John still meets with his mentor on a regular basis, and now he mentors others, as well. Though he has experienced great success, he still felt like something was missing. While his company has made a complete turnaround, he felt a little empty inside.

On his fortieth birthday, John realized what had been missing. That morning, he had an appointment for a relaxing massage from Janine, the newest employee at his usual spa. While he was talking with her, he asked, "How many hours a day do you work here?"

"Not a single one," she answered.

Abruptly jerking his head, John looked at her and asked, "What do you mean? You're working now."

"Hardly," she countered in a soothing tone. "I love what I do, so it's not work to me. When I was young, someone once asked me what I would do for a living if I could do it for free. After many jobs and much thought, this is the living I chose. It's the perfect career for me, and it keeps me balanced."

"Balanced, you say?" John inquired with sincere interest.

"Yes. I've found that the secret to happiness is having all the parts of your life in order—physical, spiritual, emotional, mental, and of course, financial."

"Well, that's pretty deep. It's something I'm going to have to think about," he said.

"You do that, but for now just relax," Janine replied as she kneaded his shoulders.

The birthday boy enjoyed the rest of his therapy session. When it was over, he sat up and asked Janine one last question, "I'm curious. Why do you like massage therapy so much? I mean, what do you get out of it?"

"Massage is only part of my personal secret to happiness. I've traveled the world, and I've decided that my passion lies in business, which is what really brings me here."

Wondering what she meant, John flashed a confused look her way.

"Let me explain," she elaborated. "Over the past eleven years, I've been managing spas all over the world, from Bombay to Jamaica. I've learned everything about operating spas—from saunas to exercise rooms to mineral pools to marketing the business—and I've decided I want to open a spa of my own one day soon."

"That's great," John said enthusiastically, "but it still doesn't explain why you're here, working on me now."

"Well, the only part missing from my complete knowledge of the industry was doing the massages myself, so I took classes to be a licensed therapist. Now, I'm putting into practice what I've learned. The final step is to open my own location. This way, I will be able to relate to everyone who works with me, and I can fill any position if need be. It makes plenty of sense to me."

John suddenly realized the similarities between what she was saying and what his mentor talked about so many lessons before.

Leaving the club, there was a renewed zest to his step that he hadn't felt in years. The next day, he showed up at the office, waving as he walked by the first-floor receptionist, Rhonda (who now has her own assistant), and got into the elevator, where he chatted warmly with everyone on board. As he walked through the brightly painted hallway into his office, he glanced up to see the message scrolling on the electronic LED sign—*Make a Positive Impact.*

He stopped to speak with his assistant, Mary, to see how her weekend went and ask how her oldest son did in his ballgame the night before. When they finished catching up, John walked into his office. As he took his seat behind his smaller, more functional desk, which was now decorated with photos of his family and friends, he called out, "Mary, would you please come in here? I would like to discuss something with you."

"What's up, J.B.?" Mary asked as she strolled into his office and took a seat.

"I'm giving a month's notice today. I'm leaving the firm, and I wanted you to be the first to know. It's time I followed my passion, as everyone keeps saying, and I'm ready to take a chance to pursue what I love."

"That's wonderful, John," she smiled. "While you'll certainly be missed, I'm happy for you. If I might ask, what are you going to pursue?"

"Right there," he said with pride in his voice as he pointed to a neatly framed picture—the same picture of him and his father in front of the old movie house that had once been tucked in a corner, only now the black and white image was blown up and in full color.

"I've always hoped to follow in my grandfather's footsteps, and now that I have the ability and have found the true desire to do so, I believe I will. Here's one of the best parts—I'm recommending to the board that you take over my position. You've learned everything I do here and, to be honest, you've done most of the work for me over these past few years. It's only fair that you get recognized for all you've accomplished for this company."

Astonished, Mary stood up and walked around the desk to hug the supervisor she had grown to respect over the years. "Thank you so much, J.B. I'm deeply touched by your faith in me."

Four weeks later, Mr. Bishop left his position, and even though he felt some anxiety about his next quest, he knew it would be worth it. A broad smile spread across his face as he realized that he was about to do something most people only dream of: *Wake up and live the life you love!*

And that's exactly what he did. John's new business was more successful than he had dared to hope, and he knew his grandfather would have been so proud. Newly renovated, the theater became the talk of the town once again. The formerly rundown and neglected cinema was now a state-of-the-art facility that everyone wanted to attend.

John had never felt so proud or so fulfilled. He was pursuing his ultimate dream, coincidentally in an industry needed by his greatest ally, Oscar Cams. While the two men had formed a mutually respected friendship, they also formed a business partnership that created more abundance in each of their lives than they could have ever imagined. Working fantastically together, they opened new theaters all over the state and created one of the largest chains that had ever graced the land.

During an interview for a local newspaper, a reporter asked John the secret to his success. He replied, "Most people in the business think— what's the *least* I can pay to get someone to work for me? Now, thanks to some great wisdom bestowed unto me, my new attitude is: *What's the <u>most</u> I can afford to share to get someone to work with me?*

"I only surround myself with the very best people—the Tiger Woods of accounting, the Bill Gates of sales and marketing, and the Oprah Winfrey of human resources. Then, since I've hired only the best, I allow them to do their jobs, treat them like they're part of my family, and share the profits with them.

"And you know what? I don't even have to manage them because they're the best in their field, and they manage their departments and themselves. In return for this relationship, they treat the company as if it were their own. And it is. It really belongs to all of us—we're all involved in its success."

Fascinated, the reporter asked if John faced tough times when getting started.

"Of course I did," John replied. "That's part of life. However, since I was so focused on the end result and not so caught up in the little things that happened along the way, I never got caught up in the moguls."

"The moguls?" asked the reporter.

"Yes, the moguls. Imagine that I'm standing in my skis atop a mountain, getting ready to race to the bottom. I'm focused on getting to the finish line. Now, along the way, there are moguls, trees, black ice, wind, and bitter cold weather. You know—obstacles! But since I know they're coming, they don't really bother me. Other people get caught up in them. They fall down, get up, and fall down again. Unfortunately, at this point—cold, wet, and maybe hurt—most *stay* down. Yet when I fall down, no matter how many times, I don't let it affect my attitude, stop my progress, or—most important— make me lose my focus on the desired end result."

"Getting to the fireplace in the ski lodge," the reporter chimed in.

"You got it," John laughed.

"Let me ask you," pressed the reporter. "How did you make your first million?"

"As strange as it is, I did it by *not* chasing millions. I did it by finding something I was *passionate* about and then pursued that with everything I had. In the book, *The Millionaire Mentor*, you'll find one of my favorite quotes: *When you do what you love and love what you do, you'll have success your whole life through.* That's why I tell everyone I mentor to find their passion and then money will follow—like it did for singers like Kelly Clarkson, actors like Jim Carrey and George Clooney. And then there are the entrepreneurs who everyone knows, like Ted Turner, Steve Jobs, Bill Gates, and Donald Trump. And let's not forget the great legends like Walt Disney and so many others. These people focused on their passion, and the money chased after them."

"Why do you say there's no such thing as a slacker?" the reporter continued to probe.

"Well, it's simple really. If you lined up *everyone* in a row and asked if they wanted to be financially independent, not too many would pipe up and say they'd rather live in a box under a bridge, right?

"I think of it this way. Think of the laziest oaf you know, that guy who never gets off the sofa except to get another bag of chips. You know who I mean. Then imagine walking into the room and asking if he wants to go to the big game with you. What would happen? He'd jump up, shower, put on his favorite gear, and off to the stadium you'd go!

"Well, there are hundreds of people who literally get to do just that every day—the sportscasters, the refs, even the towel boys are doing something that most only dream about. They're actually loving and living the life they choose. They're *passionate* about their work, so like I said before, they're really *never* working at all."

"Why should a person start his or her own business? Isn't starting your own business a very risky thing to do?" the reporter asked.

"Let me ask you a question. Didn't the people you work for now at some time start their own business—where *you* now find you have a *job* working for *them*? You might call it a job, but I like to think of it as a J.O.B.—and we *all* know what that stands for—Just Over Broke! The only difference between you and them is that they put their fears aside and took action. Now, what's stopping you?"

When the articles appeared in the local newspaper, the whole town came to know the real John Bishop.

welcome to the family!

As the days, months, and years passed, so did our friend, Mr. Cams, Sr. Though he was deeply missed, the tears shed on his behalf were happy ones in celebration of the rich, full life of an endearing man who touched the hearts of many.

John stayed in touch with the aging Oscar and Ellen Cams and became like a son to them, which was a true blessing, as they never had children of their own. They became a family, spending holidays together and helping each other's companies and charities become the best they could be.

When John left Mr. Cams's office so many years before, he decided to turn things around for both himself and others. Five years later, he'd become the talk of the town—this time, because of the wonderful things he did for the community, while creating his own corporation around his ultimate passion.

Today, his business was better than ever, and the relationships he developed had become legendary throughout his city. Everyone wanted to meet this man so they, too, could learn the secrets to his success.

When he arrived at his mentor's office for a visit, like he'd done so very many times before, John was greeted by the same receptionist he met on that very first day.

"Mr. Cams will see you now," Ellen said in a mock-professional manner.

"Nonsense," John said, rounding the desk to give her a warm and gentle hug.

"My, how you've changed since we first met, John Bishop. Now, you go in there," Ellen directed as she pointed to the door and patted him on the back.

John entered the room to see Oscar staring out his big window, more content and at ease that he'd ever seen him before.

"What's the story, morning glory?" John asked in a singsong fashion.

"It's time we had a little talk," the mentor simply said. "Walk with me."

Hearing the seriousness in his friend's tone, John shot him a look of concern as the two walked out the door and down the familiar hallway.

"Go inside," Oscar directed as he held back the curtain to the Wall of Fame room he'd first introduced the younger VP to so long ago.

As John walked into the room, he noticed that a space on the wall now had *his* picture on it. In a daze, he murmured, "What's going on?"

"Congratulations," announced Ellen as she quietly walked to stand beside her husband. Giving John's shoulders a squeeze, she said, "We want you to have this."

"Have what?" John asked, confused.

Oscar turned to him proudly and said, "You've become more than a friend to us over the years. Your actions have proven more about your character than words could ever describe. You're a different person than you were when you first walked through our doors. And, John, I think you know how much we admire you. Now that it's time for us to retire and move on, we want to offer you our corporation. Combined with your company, you'll be an unstoppable force. But more important, we believe in our hearts that you'll know what to do with such power."

Stunned, felt a sense of déjà vu. Like a deer in the headlights, he stood in bewilderment and awe as he grasped the enormity of what he'd just heard. After a moment or two of silence, he said solemnly and sincerely, "It will be my honor, my privilege, and my promise to live up to the expectations and dreams you've worked so diligently to create. The first thing I'd like to do as the new CEO is request that the two of you join me and head up *our* advisory board, to oversee the transition and continue to be part of something that tremendously affects the lives of so many *family members.*"

"We accept," Ellen agreed without consulting her husband. "Now, let's go celebrate!"

As the three good friends, smiling broadly, walked out of the Wall of Fame room into the factory, the electronic sign lit up and sprang to life. As John stepped into his future, he paused to read the announcement:

John Bishop

Welcome to the Family!

universal success secrets

Always maintain a positive, solution-searching attitude.

To truly succeed at anything, our chances increase when
we enjoy the task—for when we do what we love and love
what we do, we'll have success our whole life through.

The only <u>limitations</u> we really have
are those we give ourselves.
The only <u>expectations</u> we need fulfill
are those we give ourselves.

☆☆☆

There is nothing as powerful as a positive attitude,
and nothing as detrimental as a negative one.

Morally speaking, if we have to wonder whether
something is right or wrong, chances are, it's wrong.

When we focus on other people's success,
ours is sure to follow.

Live your word—lead by example.

Share. (Wealth + Information + Glory + Success)

☆☆☆

The best chance of reaching a goal
is to simply give yourself one to reach.

☆☆☆

Observe every obstacle as a learning experience.
The greater the challenge, the greater the reward.

☆☆☆

Do the hardest thing first—the rest will be easy.

☆☆☆

Treat others the way THEY want to be treated.

Few great accomplishments have ever been achieved alone;
seek support from those with talents that exceed your own.

We *are* the reflection of the five people we associate
with the most, and our income is the average
of those five people.
Choose your friends wisely.

A dream written down with a date becomes a GOAL.
A goal broken down into steps becomes a PLAN.
A plan backed by ACTION makes your dream come true.

We learn more about someone's character on *one* bad day,
than on *all* their good days put together. The true measure
of all great leaders is how well they weather storms.

☆☆☆

It's better to invest time doing what pleases you, rather
than to waste time trying to please everyone else.

☆☆☆

In the end, the extent of our own success
will be measured by the accomplishments
that we have helped create in *others.*

Having *potential* simply means that you possess
talents and abilities that you are *not* applying.

Things are the way you *think* they are because
you *think* they are that way. Our perception
determines our experience.

share your success stories

In the time it takes for a short flight, you can read, absorb, and become inspired by this entire book, which has impacted the lives of many around the world. We encourage you to pass it on by sharing your thoughts, ideas, and excitement with others. In under one hour, you can make a world of difference in the lives of others by telling them how the information in this book made a positive impact on you. We call it the 57-minute challenge.

So, tell us ... how did this book make a **Positive Impact** on you?

about Greg S. Reid

For over 25 years, Greg has inspired millions of people to take personal responsibility to step into the potential of their greatness, and, as such, his life of contribution has been recognized by government leaders, a foreign Princess, as well as luminaries in education, business, and industry.

Mr. Reid has been published in over 100 books, including 32 bestsellers in 45 languages. Titles, such as *Stickability: The Power of Perseverance; The Millionaire Mentor,* and *Three Feet from Gold: Turn Your Obstacles into Opportunities,* have inspired countless readers to understand that the most valuable lessons we learn are also the easiest ones to apply.

Greg is known best for being Founder of Secret Knock, a Forbes and Inc. magazine top-rated event focused on partnership, networking, and business development.

He is the producer of the Oscar-qualified film, *Wish Man,* based on the creator of the Make A Wish Foundation.

For his work in mentoring youth in his hometown of San Diego, Mr. Reid was honored by the White House, where a former President commended Greg for positively working with youth through a local mentorship program.

And if that is not enough, recently Greg was honored with the star on the infamous Las Vegas Walk of Stars.

To learn more, visit Gregreid.com

about Charlie "Tremendous" Jones

For more than fifty years, thousands of audiences around the world experienced nonstop laughter as "Tremendous" Jones shared his ideas about life's most challenging situations in business and at home. Two of his speeches, "The Price of Leadership" and "Where Does Leadership Begin?" have been enjoyed by millions.

A publisher, motivator, and humorist, Charles "T" Jones was president of Executive Books and the author of the bestselling book, *Life is Tremendous*.

about Tracey C. Jones

Author, speaker, veteran, international leadership expert, publisher, and podcaster Tracey C. Jones is the President of Tremendous Leadership, a legacy business founded by her father, Charlie "Tremendous" Jones in 1965. Dr. Jones is a graduate of the United States Air Force Academy, a decorated veteran who served in the First Gulf War and Bosnian War, earned an MBA in Global Management, and a Ph.D. in Leadership Studies. She is a passionate lifelong learner whose career spans top positions in four major industries from the military to high tech to defense contracting and publishing. Tracey is the author of ten titles, five of which are children's books that use her rescue pets to teach character development to our next generation of emerging leaders. She is driven to help others discover their intrinsic greatness and give them the resources to ignite the world.

To learn more about Tracey, please visit traceycjones.com and tremendousleadership.com.

This edition of *Positive Impact* honors

Charlie "Tremendous" Jones

and Jack Mates,

who have both made a positive impact

on the lives of many.

They may be gone, but their message lives on.

Make a positive impact on those around you,

and you, too, will be tremendous!

Made in the USA
Monee, IL
04 August 2021